Does This Date

Make My Ass Look Big?

Does This Date
Make My Ass Look Big?

Women sharing online dating's
bottom line

Cathy Romano

Edited by Tiffany Yates-Martin
Illustrated by Dawn Gabehart
Photography by Bob Romano, Tara Gimmer

ISBN-13:978-1500765903

Book design by Maureen Cutajar
www.gopublished.com

This book is dedicated to Bob, my favorite date,
who recently shared this with me:

There is a study out about women and how they feel about their ass. The results were pretty interesting:

30% of women think their ass is too fat...

10% of women think their ass is too skinny...

The remaining 60% say they don't care, they love him, he's a good man, and they wouldn't trade him for the world.

Contents

Introduction

ACCORDING TO THE U.S. CENSUS, there are now 95.9 million unmarried people in the U.S., of which 47 percent are men and 53 percent are women. The National Center for Family and Marriage Research reports that the divorce rate for people over 50 has doubled in the past 20 years. By the year 2030, there are projected to be 800,000 divorces—annually! According to another site, Statisticbrain.com, at the start of 2014 over 41 million Americans had tried online dating. When I saw these numbers it made sense that online dating, although a relatively new phenomenon, is becoming more prevalent, and there's a lot of interest surrounding it right now. Maybe you're single and want to start dating, or maybe you're just plain curious to know what online dating is all about, whether you ever plan to do it or not. Or maybe you're like me: a married person just fascinated by hearing others' dating experiences that seem to captivate any audience and dominate conversations everywhere.

It has quickly become apparent that there is no Yelp for bad dates—but there are people out there like me, who like to listen, empathize, and cheer friends on. Being an active listener to others' experiences was not only therapeutic for both my interviewees and me, but it also made me reminisce about my old dating days—the awkwardness and excitement—and now I was a captivated audience, reliving that experience in a sense, and getting a new perspective in my fifties.

Does This Date Make My Ass Look Big: Women sharing online dating's bottom line, will take you down the path of just some of the dating stories I got from interviewing various women willing to share their experiences. At the end of each interview I would ask the same question: "Your advice for others?" Following each story, I've included their tips, while using a selection of both sweet and shocking stories to answer some dating questions, assure others they aren't the only ones who've had bad dates, and then reveal some humor and hope in it all.

According to Randomhistory.com, which is a website created by a team of history enthusiasts dedicated to providing the web's best selection of history and random topics, Internet dating statistics show that a third of online daters form a relationship, another third do not but keep trying, and the remaining third give up altogether. The women I interviewed visited various Internet dating sites with the original intent of alleviating their loneliness, reinventing and "remarketing" themselves, or just to have fun again. After being totally mesmerized by their sometimes unbelievable stories, I decided to write this book without using any real names. I felt that if more women knew others' had similar experiences, both good and bad, it would give them the hope they need to keep searching for happiness.

After clocking hundreds of hours gathering others' experiences, I selected fifteen of the best stories to share. Along with their advice, I decided to include my own editorials to some of the stories, or "my turn." I just couldn't resist making up my own version of what I would have said to have the last word. I hope you have as much fun reading this as I did interviewing, listening, laughing along with, and even crying over some of their experiences. I often found myself sitting there with my mouth wide open.

In the end, I was happy to find, and share, that there was a silver lining in every story. It was my goal in creating this book to make the sometimes discouraging and demoralizing growing digital dating scene into something light and comical for those testing, or just curious, about the Internet dating waters. I am confident that the contents that follow will give readers a glimmer of humor but also, and more important, a glimmer of hope—and finally, even a glimmer of help before, during, or after taking the online dating plunge.

—Cathy Romano
www.cathyromano.com

Ready? Set?

Dating Prep

Ten Things Dating Websites Don't Tell You

HERE ARE KEY POINTS from an article by Quentin Fottrell, author of the book *Love in a Damp Climate: The Dating Game...Irish-Style,* (QF) that appeared in the Wall Street Journal on February 10, 2013, and my additional comments. (CR)

QF: "Finding a soul mate is expensive."
CR: First there are the online dating site monthly fees, and then there's all that money spent to get ready for the dating world again. But just think about how great you are going to look, and feel, after you reinvent yourself!

QF: "Everyone is single sooner or later."
CR: AARP has even gotten into the swing of things by launching its own online dating service—it's a good fit, since 25 percent of AARP's 37 million members are single. Older—single—and wiser now!

QF: "Cupid's arrow often misses."
CR: And misses badly, but this isn't always a bad thing, as evidenced by some of the stories that follow.

QF: *"So many liars, so little time."*

CR: "He didn't look anything like his picture . . . and he didn't tell me his hair was on his back! If I'm going to get laser treatments, can't he, too?"

QF: *"And you thought Facebook was nosy."*

CR: It seems when it comes to online dating profiles, TMI may be a good thing. And more (accurate) is better than less (accurate).

QF: *"This place (every Internet dating site) is a hotbed for adulterers."*

CR: Some of the women I interviewed had "surprise" dates with married men, and the men were more surprised than anyone when they got caught!

QF: *"Don't judge a person by the photo."*

CR: How about the woman who dated a guy who said he "needed to lose a few pounds" and showed up tipping the scales at 300? A bit more "food" for thought: "If you tell the truth, you don't have to remember anything"—Mark Twain.

QF: *"Keep a close eye on your wallet."*

CR: Seniors aren't the only target for scams . . . it appears singles are, too. (Easy to spot though—it's the person asking you to wire funds before asking you to dinner.)

QF: *"Objectification: It's what's for dinner."*

CR: Picky, picky . . . but it's what filters are supposed to do. Why waste your valuable time on those who don't meet your checklist? The checklists that some women I interviewed use are invaluable. They help them know who they are and not just who they want.

QF: *"Endless love—or endless chat?"*

CR: These dating websites can be addicting, a time burner and a complete waste of time. Meeting face-to-face is the only way to know for sure. (And the sooner you "face" this fact, the better!)

The Handy-Dandy
Internet Profile Decoder

This decoder could come in handy when you're reading the profiles of potential dates.

WHAT HIS PROFILE SAYS	WHAT IT *REALLY* MEANS
Entrepreneur	Out of work
Consultant	Out of work
Between Jobs	Broke *and* out of work
Exercises 1 to 2 x per week	Watches sports 4 to 5 x per week
Somewhat spiritual	St. Starbucks or St. Mattress?
Loves to wear hats	Bald
Loves football games	Loves beer
Loves to cuddle	Bullshitter
Stocky build	Fat
Just under six feet tall	Five' seven" (on his toes)
Likes independent women	You're buying
Sensitive	Cries when his team loses
Still has lots of hair	On his back

Go Out!

*15 anonymous dating stories —
the good, the bad, and the funny*

Breast of Friends

MAGGIE'S PROFILE:

I'm a 60-year-old woman, seeking men ages 60 to 68 within a 50-mile radius from where I live. I enjoy life and I laugh easily. I'm outgoing and also fairly well educated and have a professional career and own my own business. I became much blonder recently, although born a brunette, which explains some of my older pictures. I also love my family and friends, and my only regret is that I haven't met you. I'll probably always be the definition of a fair-weather golfer, because if it's over 90 degrees out or less than 40, or if it's raining, there's no way I'm going out on that course! Yes, that's a problem in Texas. But on the other hand, I'm game to meet you at the nineteenth hole no matter what the weather.

HER STORY:

Maggie divorced her husband of twenty years and moved to another state for a new start. There she met a man and had a ten year relationship with him. When that ended after the realization it wasn't going anywhere, Maggie decided to move to Austin to be close to family. In the two years she lived there, she had many dates as a result of Internet dating but none were meaningful. She finally realized that she just didn't click with the local men she was meeting. "Internet dating," she believes, "is a microcosm of the city you live in." Maggie knew it was time to go back to her hometown and try her luck there. Once relocated, she had no problem meeting men, and met Jack in a bar while out with friends that resulted in a two year relationship. It eventually ended when she learned he had stayed on Match.com the whole time they dated, even though they decided to be exclusive. In fact, he eventually confessed he had a girlfriend on the side; once she learned this, Maggie ended the relationship but they remained friends, despite her disappointment in him. One night she got a call that Jack died of a heart attack in his sleep. This news crushed her, as their friendship was important to her, even after their break-up.

A year after the loss of Jack, she went on Match.com and started dating a man, Doug, mostly because he was the type of man who every woman wanted to be with: He was handsome, charming, and sexy. Unfortunately, she paid a price for dating a "looker" as he had other flaws which she discovered when she opted for a mastectomy due to a family history of breast cancer. She was devastated to see the look of shock on his face when he saw her new breasts and tattooed nipples. It sealed her suspicions that he was not the man for her, and she finally had the courage to end the relationship with this man and send him packing. Now he could be someone else's problem.

She had corresponded casually with another man on Match.com while she was dating Doug and she decided to pursue him more since she was now single again. He was truly the man of her dreams: Jerry was tall, smart, handsome, successful, caring, and romantic. He was the total package. They dated exclusively for months, or so she thought, but in the end he went back to an old girlfriend he'd been seeing the whole time he was dating her and finally told her he had to decide between Maggie and the other woman. He chose the other woman, and she was devastated. Maggie and Jerry continued to keep in touch and remained friends, and although difficult it turned out to be advantageous to her. Because she had also been friends with Jerry during her mastectomy ordeal and although her boyfriend at the time proved to be unsupportive, it was Jerry who came through for her.

He solidified their strong friendship when he called her often to check on her, sent her flowers, and then did something out of the ordinary: He took her out to dinner and gave her a get-well card that had a large check in it. He said he knew that she was self-employed and he wanted to help pay for her medical bills. He helped her not only financially but, more important, emotionally, as he told her she was still the most beautiful woman he'd ever met. He assured her that despite the reaction she'd received from her ex-boyfriend this was indeed the truth. Their dinner that night ended with a spontaneous romantic interlude that gave Maggie the confidence she needed and confirmation that she still, indeed, was a beautiful, sexy woman.

Today they are still great friends, and Jerry is no longer dating the other woman. Maggie has accepted that he loves her in his own way, as best as he can feel love for a woman without having an exclusive relationship. She has spent the past years focusing on the good and not the bad. It has been her discovery that men who are on Internet dating sites are just as flawed as anyone else—including her—and if you can't overlook and accept that, then you may never end up dating anyone. Maggie says she would marry Jerry in a heartbeat but unfortunately he doesn't feel the same way. But for now, having him in her life as her "bosom buddy" ironically still makes her the envy of her married friends. Most say they would give anything to have a man like this in their lives who, despite the lack of commitment to Maggie in the ideal sense, seems to not only know what she wants, but delivers it, too!

MAGGIE'S SILVER LINING:

Although presently not married, she attributes her online dating success to all the homework she did toward it: Checking out other women's profiles to see who her "competition" was, creating an honest profile, and making clear what her deal breakers were. This list included education, height, humor, religion, and zero tolerance for overcritical people. There was no compromising if any of these characteristics fell "short"—especially height! To this day, Maggie is grateful for Internet dating, even though she has lost a good friend and has endured pain and disappointment from some of the other men she has met. Ultimately online dating for her has produced important male friendships, all whom have had major impacts on her life and made it more meaningful. Her positive attitude towards dating has made her the kind of woman men want to be around.

MAGGIE'S BOTTOM LINE:
Approach Internet dating by focusing on the good things you will get from it. Nothing ventured, nothing gained.

Just Beat It

ALICE'S PROFILE:

A 50-year-old, fun and energetic, newly divorced mother of three older children, I don't need to be married again, but I am looking for a monogamous relationship with someone who will make me laugh. I desire a nonsmoker, a professional, and someone who is fashionable. I am a social drinker and I'd like it if you were one, too.

HER STORY:

Alice found herself in a sexless, lifeless marriage after 25 years, with three kids, but was still willing to put forth the effort to make the marriage work. After years of being the only one trying to salvage their fractured relationship, she finally got angry and frustrated enough to grant her husband a divorce.

She waited for about a year and a half before she tried Internet dating, because as time went on and as she talked to other girlfriends, she knew she wasn't going to meet anyone at the grocery store. She noticed that many of her friends were trying Internet dating and it was always the main topic of their discussions, so she thought that she'd give it a try. Alice found herself excited to correspond with potential dates online, but waited about six months after she first signed up to go out on a real date. She picked her very first date mostly because of his physical appearance—she was now feeling a bit desperate and just wanted to date anyone and get started!

Jay e-mailed her and suggested they meet downtown for a drink. Alice walked into the bar, her first date as a woman in her mid-fifties in more than 26 years, and felt a bit awkward, but also somewhat excited. Jay, who seemed like Mr. Nice Guy at first, was very handsome and liked to drink—something they had in common in their profiles. In fact, he and Alice both enjoyed drinking that night, and probably too much, which resulted in their mutual bad decision to continue with the date elsewhere. As he picked up the tab, Alice had convinced herself that this was a nice man and the date was going well. He seemed to pass all the first tests. That was good enough for her, especially since she didn't really have high expectations yet. Jay mentioned that he had invited a few friends over and wanted her to come over to his house and meet them. So Alice drove her own car and followed "Mr. Nice Guy" home.

When they got to his house there were a few people there, but by then Alice and Jay clearly were not interested in mingling with them—or anyone else, for that matter. Instead, they settled on the couch while the others were in the kitchen and started to kiss. That led them to his bedroom, where they took their intimacy to the next level. Alice was thrilled to be having sex again, and especially with such a good looking man, after being deprived of intimacy for so long. But as things progressed, she had a weird sense that they were not alone. Her suspicions were right, as she discovered when she cocked her head back while lying in a precarious position on the bed, and saw another man, naked, in the corner of the room as an "active" bystander, really "handing it" to himself. She screamed, got up, and demanded an explanation.

Mr. Nice Guy said he thought Alice might like this sort of group setup with his eager roommate, and with that, out of both fear and rage, she left the house, wearing nothing but a look of shock, with all her clothes clutched in her arms. She jumped in her car, drove away naked for about a block, stopped and put her clothes on, and kept driving until things started looking familiar and she could get back home to her "boring" life.

MY TURN:

(Here's what I would have said as I was bolting out the bedroom) I'm really glad your roommate is here with us because he just gave me a great idea—now it's my turn to *beat it!*

ALICE'S SILVER LINING:

The disastrous date was the jolt Alice needed to rediscover herself and get her act together. She has learned over time that liking herself and becoming her own person is better than searching for a match online too soon to make herself complete. She currently landed a good job, has found her own identity and has boosted her confidence because of it, and is concentrating on just herself for the first time in her life. Alice is so fulfilled presently that she is in no hurry to get back to dating anytime soon and is off the market altogether.

ALICE'S BOTTOM LINE:

Help improve your odds of successful dating by waiting until you get your act together before you even start. ✦

Two Can Play That Game

VALERIE'S PROFILE:

I am a 58-year-old female looking for a family man who is attractive, financially independent, and likes kids. I'm looking for a new best friend, a soul mate, the man of my dreams! I will not rush to find the right person; I'm going to be cautious. My life is full, I'm happy, but I have room in my life for a new friend and new adventures. I am kind, loving, honest, attractive, and fun! I'm looking for someone who's well educated, smart, honest, fun, and has integrity and compassion. Someone who works hard but is willing to play hard as well. Some-one who loves to talk and laugh, has a sense of humor, and is as comfortable attending a gala as walking the dogs. (Okay, almost as comfortable.) I'm not your greatest cook, and would love to take cooking lessons someday, maybe even in Italy.

HER STORY:

Valerie suddenly found herself a widow at age 55 after being married for almost 30 years. Although hesitant to start dating again too soon, she knew she was still young and had a long life ahead of her to share with someone. She had many girlfriends who were dating, and thought she'd give it a try and put herself out there as well when the time was right. She had heard from other single friends that relying on friends to set you up with someone was unrealistic and she didn't want to be set up with someone else's ex-husband in her "hood." Because of this, the best answer for her was online dating to broaden her search, which meant looking for potential dates in other states as well.

She got a real boost from all the attention she got immediately from her profile on Match.com. The winks and comments gave her confidence and, she would admit, gave her something to look forward to every day. Little by little, this made her stronger. Her first date, about six months after her husband had passed away, was uneventful, but she was proud that she could take the first step, overcome her vulnerability, and start the healing process.

She had one or two boring dates over a glass of wine at bars close to her home to start off with, but it was a certain man, Ken, who really caught her attention. For several months he provided the emotional connection she never had with her husband. He was a good listener, seemed like a wonderful father, from his description of his interaction with his children, and he was the first man she found appealing from his picture and profile. Their correspondence led to an eventual meeting, as he was coming to town on a business trip, and he suggested they finally meet.

Valerie was very excited for the first time in a long time. She met him downtown at his hotel bar, and when she arrived, he was just as attractive as his picture and was very charming. The first thing on his agenda was to get a drink at the lobby bar. From there, they decided to have some dinner close by his hotel. Ken ate very little of his meal and seemed both anxious and distracted. When they got back to his hotel, she suggested they go to the lobby bar and listen to some music. It was then that he got right to the point and told her that he would rather she come up to his room. Valerie told him it was way too soon for that, and that she wanted to get to know him better. He persisted and wouldn't let it go. She was so disappointed in his behavior, since he had fit so many of her criteria and she'd had such high hopes for finding a soul mate from online dating. But she stuck to her guns and told him it was time for the date to end.

Ken walked her to her car, but again, he had other plans. He jumped in the passenger's seat next to her and asked her to come up to his room. Again, she resisted. "Okay," he finally said, "you want to get to know me better? Here's a game I like to play that will help do just that—

we both get to ask three questions about each other." Ken went first, asking her some very superficial questions. She couldn't even remember the specific ones, but she answered all of them and purposely stretched out her answers. Then it was her turn. She hadn't even gotten one question out when Ken blurted, "Game's over; *now* can we go to my room?" She was dumbfounded and told him to leave. As Ken was getting out of her car, Valerie heard him mumble something about having to spend the rest of the night, alone, in his hotel room. Before she drove away, he did ask her to text him when she got home to make sure she arrived safely. What a considerate guy!

As instructed, she did text him to tell him she was back at home. She was a bit irritated when he texted her back to report that he was still sitting in the hotel bar, probably looking for another sucker to play his three-questions game.

MY TURN:
(Here's what I would have said as I drove away) It's obvious that you like games, so here's one I like to play, too, that also involves threes: Baseball—*and you've just struck out!*

VALERIE'S SILVER LINING:
Her date was a wakeup call for her. She is not desperate to find someone so she decided to spend her energy and time on getting her real estate license. She is still dating but is now more selective about the process, and when she meets someone who is this aggressive on the first date, she ends it on that first strike and does not wait until the third. She would tell anyone new to dating that it's worth all the disappointment and frustration to pursue a match online, because at this stage in life, she truly believes that it is the most efficient way to meet someone. Although still waiting for the perfect match, Valerie is enjoying her successful career where she is knocking it out of the ballpark!

VALERIE'S BOTTOM LINE:
Beware of men who move too fast and don't really want to know much about you.

Can't Buy Me Love

GINA'S PROFILE:

I love tennis, gardening, and the outdoors. I don't have any religious preference, but my political affiliation is important. I am looking for a lifetime companion and not a short time lover. My family is very important to me, so it would have to be important to my companion as well. I love to travel and lie on a beach with a good book.

HER STORY:

Gina married her high school sweetheart after they met at a football game as freshmen and she dated him exclusively for seven years until they wed. They were married for 20 years, and it was Gina's decision to end the marriage, because she felt they had grown apart and also took each other for granted. Maybe, never having dated anyone else, she felt the overwhelming need to find out whether there was someone better out there. Her curiosity got the best of her.

At age 43, Gina was free to start dating, and the possibilities of the unknown excited her. The first man she met, through friends, was totally different from her husband, and this appealed to her. During the five years they dated, Gina was a different, more sexually alive person, and she liked feeling this way. However, she also knew in her heart that he wasn't the one, so she eventually ended it and moved on. After that, she struck out on several blind dates that her friends had set up and was persuaded by some male friends to go the digital dating route. They had both found luck and thought she could too.

Despite what her profile said, she picked up immediately in her early correspondences that some men actually assumed she wanted casual sex and that that was the only reason she'd signed up for online dating. In some weaker moments and against her better judgment, she did have a few brief sexual encounters that left her feeling empty and a bit deceived. (She had one man actually pull off his condom when they were having sex!)

Gina decided to be more selective, and continued to look for more qualified men, but noticed that the online system she registered with automatically matched her with men quite a bit older than she was. No wonder so many men married younger women, she thought, leaving women in their forties to sixties to date men many years older!

Gina was contacted by a man on Match.com who was recently divorced, and from his very first comments, she could tell he was extremely bitter. But she knew everyone has stuff that is both desirable and undesirable, so she decided to get to know this guy, despite his apparent flaws. Ward said that his ex-wife didn't appreciate him and all the things he gave her. This should have been a huge red flag, but she ignored it at first. After the first date, Gina received a huge flower arrangement the next day with a card that read, "Missing you already." A few more dates followed—and so did the gifts. It was almost embarrassing how nice they were! After dating for just a few weeks, she mentioned to Ward casually that she was going to Mexico with her daughter and granddaughter for some much anticipated family time, and he showed up at her house with more gifts, now for the entire family.

Gina was actually sort of relieved to be getting away from this guy because she sensed the relationship was a bit one-sided and her feelings were not the same as Ward's apparently were. She was mostly looking forward to relaxing on a white sandy beach without a male anywhere in sight. You can imagine Gina's disbelief, well into a good book while lying on the warm sand, when she was approached by a cabana boy, who handed her a note: "You look good in that bathing suit. Please come meet me at the bar." Gina was not flattered at all by this, but instead had a sick feeling in her stomach. She looked over at the bar, and sure enough, there was Ward—Daddy "Ward" bucks—smiling at her. He had followed her on her family vacation to Mexico! She told the cabana boy to tell Ward that she would talk to him, but not until later. She left him drinking alone at the bar and headed up to her room to decompress.

In her room, she came up with a game plan. She called Ward's room and left a message for him to meet her in the lobby bar at a certain time. When she saw him, she let him know immediately that she was very upset by his stalking. His defense was that he thought it was a great idea, and he even ran it by his own daughter who also agreed. Needless to say, she told him he had used very poor judgment and he needed to go back home so she could continue her own vacation alone and in peace.

MY TURN:
(Here's the note I would have handed to the cabana boy) Sorry that you had to come such a long way to discover you can't buy me love—or even a margarita!

GINA'S SILVER LINING:
Although it was her idea to end her marriage after being out in the dating world, she has a new appreciation for her ex-husband and what they had. With no hope for reconciliation, she has moved on and can offer advice to others whether they're married or dating: Make an effort to be spontaneous, be more experimental in the sex department, and plan lots of date nights.

GINA'S BOTTOM LINE:
Beware of men who bash their ex-wives/dates and who bear too many gifts, too soon.

Teach Your Children Well

SARA'S PROFILE:

I am a 52-year-old woman, divorced with kids, who is self-employed. I love camping, coffee, and conversation. I like to exercise three to four times a week, my political views are middle-of-the-road, and my faith is important to me, because it plays a huge role in my daily decisions. I am looking for someone who has a high IQ, is easy to get along with, has a positive outlook, and is patient and considerate toward others. I want someone who is passionate about making a difference, and I won't settle for anything less.

HER STORY:

Sara and Ross were married for 20 years and had three kids. Sara felt that Ross wasn't the right partner from the beginning, and the issues that they both brought to the marriage fed on one another. Their early years were characterized by a constant state of financial and emotional turmoil, and eventually it spilled over onto the children who were aware of the tension and started showing it by being defiant at home and in school. Things got so bad that thoughts of ending the marriage were creeping into Sara's dreams. One night as she was falling asleep, the last thought she had was how tragic it was to live in such a horrible set of circumstances as theirs for the rest of her life, without any hope of things getting better. Although they had been going to counseling for a while to work things out, it was going nowhere. That night, Sara had a vivid dream about her and Ross separating after she sought the advice of an individual counselor who convinced her that she and her husband were on different paths and divorce, for them, was the only answer.

As Sara was waking up that morning, the dream still fresh in her mind, she felt a tremendous peace come over her. It was time to take the first step to end the marriage. Her heart and mind were both made up, and she could never go back to what they had. She told Ross that morning that the marriage was over, and in 18 months, the divorce was final and she was finally free.

Fairly soon after her divorce, Sara's friends wanted to set her up with guys, but she was not interested at all. But a family wedding she attended, where her brother motivated her to get started, did the trick. Being the successful business owner she was, she went into online dating like it was a job, and she was on a mission to land a good one. Her belief was that the more times she put a hook in the water, the better chance she had at catching a fish, and not just any fish but the best one. So she "power-dated." She had 17 dates in two weeks. She wasted no time dismissing the bad dates right away. She began to view Internet dating as a way to find out who she really was and what she really wanted.

She ended up with two long-term relationships before landing the "big one." When her first two relationships ended (they didn't quite hit the mark and she knew it), she used each as an opportunity to tweak her profile, making her searches more specific, her photos more current, her mission more exact. She often made the first move to contact potential prospects that met her criteria, and was the first to "wink" (match.com's term for showing interest in someone). While dating, Sara made a pact with herself never to settle for less than she deserved again, as she continued her search for true love.

It was when she expanded her ideal age criteria a few years that she found Peter, the man of her dreams. He was only a few years older than she was but that was okay because they connected right from the start. They even found themselves sending e-mails to each other at the same time! Their first date, a short lunch, turned into an entire afternoon of conversation. And when they decided this first date needed an "extension" they both blurted out the same restaurant to move to, at the exact same time. Peter and Sara have been going strong ever since, and Sara has never been happier.

SARA'S SILVER LINING:

Sara always regretted putting her children through unsuccessful relationships but she felt she scored a major victory when she found out from a friend of hers that her daughter had broken up with her boyfriend. When she asked her daughter about it, she said "I wanted more for myself, Mom, just like you have shown me, and I will never again settle for anything less." (She's taught her children well, no doubt.)

SARA'S BOTTOM LINE:

Look at Internet dating like looking for a job. Your success will be directly linked to the effort and time you put in it.

Broadsided

CARLA'S PROFILE:

I am a 5'7" attractive, conservative woman looking for a Christian man with wit, integrity, and humor. I want someone who has his own identity and a lot going on. I am someone my friends consider friendly, confident, and compassionate. I have no children at home, and I have a successful career and consider myself someone who is very stable.

HER STORY:

Carla was married for about 15 years and divorced in her late forties. She waited for two years after she was divorced to start dating. She had no problem at all getting dates, but set some strict guidelines for herself: The first date could last only an hour, she did not give out her last name, and she didn't go over to a date's house.

She found the first guys she met were very open and aggressive about wanting intimacy right away. One man she met for lunch, and before they had even ordered he looked across the table directly at her chest, and said, "I can see you really like me." "No," she said, in a very offended tone, "it's just very *cold* in here!"

She really wondered why some men wanted to "make mad passionate love" to her within 5 minutes of their meeting? One date seemed to think he could rub her leg and kiss her right off the bat, which had her totally *tongue tied* —which was perhaps his goal, not hers. This only led her to believe that there were other women out there who did "put out" too soon, ruining it for the conservative ones, like Carla, who were on a slower track. But in her quest for a suitable match, she kept on dating and stuck to her rules.

She eventually met a man who appeared to be a successful businessman in real estate. Gary was very attractive and attentive to her. Their first date was at a coffee shop, and when they said good-bye, she thought it was strange that he had a camera. In looking back, she thought it was even stranger that he wanted to take her picture, but she obliged him. She found him charming—so charming that she even agreed to have dinner with him later that night. That dinner led to more dates, and they shared a meal or two almost every day and night for weeks. The camera kept coming out after every date as well, and Carla finally sensed that something was just not right.

Other things were not adding up after he shared information with her about his business deals. This led her to the Internet to do some research. Carla was a bit shocked at her discoveries that he was a phony, especially the one where she learned he was married! She confronted Gary, and when she did, he revealed that his wife was teaching abroad for a major university; his defense was that he used her absence as an opportunity to do research for his book project on Internet dating. Needless to say, that was the last meal they had together, which closed that chapter of his book forever!

MY TURN:
(Here's what I would have told him) Let me get this straight: While your wife was teaching abroad, you thought you could date a broad? Well let me *broadside* you with this: YOU'RE BUSTED!

CARLA'S SILVER LINING:
In going forward, she took her naivety from dating the con artist to become quite the expert at screening dates.

CARLA'S BOTTOM LINE:
Before going out on that first date, do as much homework on the person you can by accessing all the resources that are currently available. When in doubt, (background) check him out?

Match, Interrupted

ZOE'S PROFILE:

I am a recently divorced woman with red hair and an athletic body style. I have conservative views, am not religious, and am a social drinker. I am a people person and love to be around people. I want someone with conservative views, not necessarily over-the-top, but who would be a good family man. I don't have any kids of my own and may be interested in someone who already has kids, or even having kids of my own, although that's not my priority. I do love golf and motorcycles and hope those interest you as well.

HER STORY:

Zoe, in her late thirties, was newly divorced after a short marriage. She immediately took to the Internet to heal her wounds and put herself out there again but was not having any luck on the first go around. She decided to become a bar hopper instead, going out almost every night. This wasn't the most productive way to meet a soul mate, and besides, it was also a bit embarrassing, since she eventually knew where all the best happy-hour deals were in Austin and she was on a first name basis with every bartender!

Zoe decided to go back to online dating to find a match, and although she preferred meeting someone without children, since she had none, she realized most of the men she'd met had them. Using a friend's observation that she might be limiting her dates by preferring only men without children, she decided to revamp her profile to include this group of potential men to help expand her search.

Barry, a single dad, indeed caught her attention. They decided to meet at a local bar on a date that she will never forget, November 15. Zoe and Barry were both shocked that neither looked like their photo, and that broke the ice when they met. The date lasted for hours, even after his "save me from this horrible date" phone call in which he assured his friend he was fine. Zoe also covered her bases by having a friend parked at a nearby bar who was sending her "check-in" texts sporadically. But by the last hour, Zoe and Barry were airing their dirty laundry and feeling quite "safe" and comfortable with each other. They walked to her car, because it was the closest, and he shook her hand and left.

Although Barry was traveling every week, he still made the effort to e-mail or call her every day. They found that they had a lot of interests and hobbies in common, and they both passed the "friends" test. Zoe even passed the family test when she met his two daughters. They dated about a month and a half, and finally the question of exclusivity came up. The pregnant pause that ensued was a clue that one of them was seeing other people, and it obviously was the one who was out of town every week. They broke up shortly after, due to their misunderstanding about dating other people. After a month sabbatical Zoe agreed to start seeing Barry again, but at a much slower pace.

Taking things slowly the second time around seemed to help seal their relationship and take it to the next level. Just a year shy of their first meeting, a wedding proposal came at the most unusual place— on a major bridge on Lake Austin during a traffic jam at rush hour. Since they weren't going anywhere, Barry talked her into getting out of the car with him, walked over to her side, got on his knees, and proposed. Fellow onlookers, also stuck on the bridge, honked with delight. Well, some were happy, and others told them to go get a hotel room somewhere! Zoe and Barry were married on November 15 on an island in the Bahamas, exactly one year after their first date.

ZOE'S SILVER LINING:

Her tenacity to stick with Internet dating, and even deciding to date the same person again when it was unsuccessful the first time, really paid off. She and Barry have been happily married, golfing and riding motorcycles now for four years, and have added a son and daughter to their family.

ZOE'S BOTTOM LINE:

Always share your dating plans with a friend or family member. Also, don't be afraid to "redate" someone even if it didn't work out the first time.

Toys R *Not* Us

DONNA'S PROFILE:

I am a 43-year-old tall blonde. I am fun-loving, active, and fit. I enjoy meeting new people and learning and experiencing new things. I am looking for a man who is age appropriate (35 to 45), who is active, excited to be alive, fun, and grounded. I prefer someone cultured and who has goals and aspirations, and is comfortable in his own skin. I don't want the 38-year-old retired weekend golfer.

HER STORY:

Donna, now 46, was married for twelve years. She admits that during her marriage, both she and her ex-husband had baggage and issues, but neither wanted to work on them, and so the marriage was doomed from the start. They had always been better friends than lovers, and although this works for some marriages, for theirs it was what finally ended it. Their sex life faded away and they were left with a friendship and nothing more. Because they both agreed the marriage was going nowhere, there was never an option of working things out, so they mutually agreed to move on.

It took Donna almost a year before she felt like dating. When she finally signed up for online dating she thought to herself, "this is good practice for getting out there, right, so what do I have to lose?" Donna enjoyed writing e-mails back and forth with men and looking at the sites, but wasn't really ready for an actual face-to-face date.

Finally, after a year of just looking, she took the plunge and got enough nerve up to go on a few dates. Her first experiences were bizarre, and she had names for each date: Dog Dude (had too many), Stoner (smoked too many), and Bondage Boy (wanted to tie the knot, literally)—just to name a few. She finally found someone in her search who didn't appear to be a loser. Doug was a fairly attractive older businessman who had even gone to her same high school, but in an earlier class. While he was shorter than she preferred, she was trying to get outside her comfort zone in case she was overlooking someone. They had a few pleasant dates over drinks, but she kept it short and sweet. Finally it was time for a longer date, so Donna agreed to go out to dinner, and they arranged that Doug would come pick her up at her house.

They had discussed going out to a nice dinner at one of her favorite restaurants so she dressed for the evening with that in mind. Doug showed up at her house and she invited him in. He was carrying a stainless-steel briefcase, but since he was a business owner, she didn't think anything of it. She poured him a glass of wine, and he said that he wanted to share something with her. He hoped she was up to the challenge and they could find a way to "use" them all. What kind of challenge was this, she thought? He put the briefcase on the table and opened it. Inside, tucked into foam slots, were six sex toys of various types, sizes, and vibration speeds. If she wasn't already shocked enough, he then asked her if she could use them all—on him! She was, needless to say, speechless. Because Donna was still relatively new to dating and was not yet confident to end the date right there, she instead suggested they go to dinner before doing anything else. Maybe this would buy her time to figure out a game plan.

They got to the restaurant and he was back to being a perfect gentleman—in public only, obviously. She finally came up with an exit plan and decided to act sick and say she needed to go home. When they got to her place she was still acting sick, but now was even starting to really feel sick, and Doug was polite enough not to press to come in. She said good-bye—forever—and locked the door behind him.

MY TURN:

(Here's what I would have said to Doug before I locked the door) You've just confirmed my dating policy which is never to date any-one with excess *baggage*!

DONNA'S SILVER LINING:

Instead of losing her dignity over the ordeal, she used it as an oppor-tunity to get stronger and apply her new integrity to all future dates. Presently, she's finally met a winner who has the type of "baggage" she can handle!

DONNA'S BOTTOM LINE:

Establish your boundaries early on and don't let anyone cross them. If they try, *always* have an exit plan and *never* lose your dignity.

Does This Date Make My Ass Look Big?

WENDY'S PROFILE:

A 40-year-old fun and energetic person, divorced mother of two boys. I don't need to be married again, but I am looking for a monogamous relationship with someone to have fun with. More specifically, I am looking for a man between the ages of 35 and 45, single of course, preferably with children, living within 30 miles of my zip code, and someone who is Christian, athletic, and professional.

HER STORY:

Wendy was in a marriage for 12 years that, over time, devolved into a friendship or partnership instead of a loving, romantic marriage. Her husband was a workaholic who was never home, making the job of raising kids much more difficult for Wendy, who found herself resentful and lonely, and the end result was a long-overdue divorce.

She was set up on a date by friends at work shortly after her divorce, but it was not a great experience for her and she was very disappointed. The blind date was such a mismatch that she wondered what her friends thought of her. She decided she'd take matters into her own hands and took the digital dating plunge.

Dale seemed like a winner to her from their brief online and phone correspondence, so they agreed to an entire weekend of dating, starting with dinner at Cheddar's, which was his suggestion. Not her dream place, but obviously it was his, as he knew all the waitresses there by name! When dinner was over he pushed for more: Dale wanted her to go back to his place and have sex with him. Wendy told him she didn't like sex that much when she was married and she really didn't like it now that she didn't have to do it. He was so mad by the rejection that he ended the date on a bad note, calling her all sorts of names as they left the restaurant parking lot. Though they had originally planned to go out the next night, she sensed neither one of them wanted to see each other again, but just to make sure she said she was busy the rest of the weekend.

Not wanting to be alone the next night, Wendy immediately enlisted a few girlfriends for support. They convinced her to go to a popular bar downtown to help cheer her up and get her over the disastrous dating experience. So out she went.

She couldn't believe it when she saw "Mr. Fast and Furious at her"—a.k.a. Dale—across the room at the same bar. Being drunk and belligerent is not a good combination; when he saw her, he immediately seized the opportunity to confront her in front of her friends. He told Wendy that although she had rejected his offer the night before, it didn't matter, because he went home and found his female neighbor willing and able, and they had sex in his hot tub. If this wasn't embarrassing enough for Wendy, he thought he would have the last word by telling her, in the crowded bar for all to hear, that she could save other men a lot of time and trouble if instead of her face, she would change her profile to a picture of her ass. And with that final blow, he left the bar.

MY TURN:
(I would have made sure I got the last word by saying this as he was leaving the bar) By opening up your mouth just now, you just proved to everyone here who the bigger *ass* really is!

WENDY'S SILVER LINING:
The rude comment that night about her body was just the motivation she needed to start working out. Wendy is thrilled with her newly toned body—and, by the way, a new classy boyfriend, too.

WENDY'S BOTTOM LINE:

Enlist in the mentor system of Internet dating because it indeed takes a "girlfriend" village to get through it. They can share your experiences with you and help keep the whole dating process light and fun instead of serious and discouraging.

Box of Chocolates

BETH'S PROFILE:

I'm a 63-year-old woman who is always on the lookout for the next adventure. I am told that I am fun to be with, a bit sassy, enthusiastic, honest, and very affectionate in a relationship. I do not want a couch potato, but want someone who could bring as much to the table to match what I am bringing. I am a positive person, and I believe in participating in life, not just observing, so I stay active physically and take care of myself. I like a direct conversation and should add that I want a relationship.

HER STORY:

Beth was married for 28 years, but as the kids got older and needed less parenting, the marriage became dull and stagnant. She was no longer willing to compromise her happiness, and her success as a real estate agent gave her the confidence to move on, alone.

This success in the world of work carried over into the new world of dating, too. Beth had so many dates that she called them her "box of chocolates"—a reference to the line in *Forrest Gump*: "Life is like a box of chocolates: You never know what you're gonna get." Beth truly never knew what she was getting, and sometimes that was a pleasant surprise, but other times it left a bad taste in her mouth! (The key for her was to know when to spit it out and try another one.) She finally got her favorite "chocolate" and has been dating Henry exclusively for almost a year now.

Beth's experience reminds us that as we get older, we get more set in our ways with our personal quirks and family dynamics. She and Henry have drawn a line in the sand when it comes to their differences and uniqueness, vowing not to judge or criticize how they talk to their own kids, how they fold their towels, or even how much mayonnaise they put in their tuna fish!

As of now, one year after their first date, Beth and Henry have a harmonious relationship. One of their keys to success was finding someone who could adapt to, instead of change for, the other. They make an effort to stay independent as they both navigate together through life in their older years.

Another key was finding someone who could keep things from getting too boring or predictable. In fact, just recently Beth and Henry went on a spur-of-the-moment surprise weekend getaway. They both really work to make sure there is always something to look forward to, as it's the key to preventing monotony in a relationship, whether you're married or not.

BETH'S SILVER LINING:
Although she thought she initially wanted marriage, she and Henry have found that their current exclusive relationship is in some ways better than marriage and they are satisfied with that. It's a commitment, but without all the temptations to criticize and change each other. The only thing they ever change is where they are going each weekend!

BETH'S BOTTOM LINE:
If the relationship is working, don't try to fix or change it.

Look No Further

ANGIE'S PROFILE:

I am a wholesome girl you should have married the first time! I am looking for a stable guy, a man with a plan and not a couch potato. I do not want any drama. I am not a jock, and don't pretend to be, but would be willing to try things if someone is willing to be patient with me. My call to action for you is that I have always wanted to learn to golf and cook and would love to have someone be my teacher.

HER STORY:

Angie had been married for 19 years before divorcing, although in hindsight she felt the marriage should have ended a lot sooner than in her late forties. She stayed in her unhappy marriage for the sake of her child, because she came from divorced parents and didn't want history to repeat itself. With the empty nest came the inevitable next step: Divorce.

Angie had been so isolated in her marriage because her unhappiness with it resulted in her lack of energy to go out and socialize with others. When she was finally single, she felt a huge sense of relief, almost a giddy feeling, over the possibilities that awaited her. She was not intimidated at all about being single; in fact, she was the opposite, and actually looked forward to it. She used the three years after her divorce to reinvent herself and create a social life with friends and experimented with new adventures the way she'd always wanted.

Although she talked about dating after enjoying being single, Angie waited another year before taking the first step to sign up online, and had a friend help coach her through the process. She had quite an assortment of oddball dates at first. One guy was from a foreign country and asked her to marry him right away and move back there with him. She had men ask her whether her breasts were real and whether she had money. One guy took her to a family reunion on their first date—way too awkward, and way too soon, and she just didn't have the courage at the time to say no. It was starting to feel creepy to Angie to be participating in online dating, so she got off, temporarily, to regroup.

After months had passed, Angie eventually came to the decision that if she was going to have success meeting a good match online, then she would have to go "all in" and take it more seriously than she did the first time. It is her belief that if your intentions and behavior are lined up, then you will find happiness. So the second time around, her attitude changed tremendously—and so did her luck. Angie updated her profile with her new approach of having enthusiasm and purpose. She was more open about the whole dating experience and realized that the first time around she was not really committed and had too many self-imposed excuses that limited her enjoyment (it was too much money, too much time, and too much energy). She even listed a "call to action" in her profile as a challenge to potential partners, asking whether someone out there could teach her to play golf or cook.

Angie's new attitude and profile soon paid off. When she first met Joe he did not set off fireworks within her heart right away, but rather it was a slow process. The deal makers were two things: She loved his friends, and he always made plans to do fun things—always! This was something that her ex-husband never did. He eventually grew on her over time. At one point, sitting across from her at dinner, Joe looked at her and said in a matter-of-fact tone, "The real problem with Internet dating is that you're always looking around because you think there is someone better out there than the one you're sitting across from." This struck a chord with Angie. Why was she fighting against this man being "the one" who could convince her to look no further? After all, he was everything she was looking for: Fun, athletic, caring, and handsome.

Before Internet dating, it seems like people took the time to get to know someone else, and didn't nitpick every little flaw. Maybe Joe was on to something: Internet dating gives us a continual supply of "new meat" and it is so much easier to throw away someone and move on to the next person. Angie decided right then and there that the man sitting across from her was a keeper.

Two years later, Joe proposed to her with a dozen long-stemmed red roses all scattered around her home, which ironically is also her place of business, where she hosts weddings. With each rose there was a clue written on a piece of paper. This clever scavenger hunt led her to the last rose, which had a sign next to it asking, "Will you marry me?" The last rose was lying on a couch and was located, appropriately, in the bridal dressing room.

ANGIE'S SILVER LINING:

She used the fact that she wasn't very athletic to her advantage. Her call to action line about learning golf helped her find a mate and she can now hold her own on the golf course, too!

ANGIE'S BOTTOM LINE:

When you do find a good thing, resist the temptation to always think there is someone better out there. Maybe your match is sitting in front of the table where you lean, instead of back home on your computer screen?

On the Move

THERESA'S PROFILE:

A friend once told me I am an "uptight hippie," and I love that description. I am looking for someone to have a blast with—but toward something committed. I'm a gigantic fan of humor of pretty much any sort (except the mean kind), with bonus points for wit and sarcasm. Life is too short for negativity, lingering anger, unresolved resentment, lack of forgiveness—and it's too cool not to appreciate every day and find the good wherever you can. I'm happier now in my life than I ever have been, and I'd love to share that with a companion.

I haven't been married yet because marriage is huge to me—it's the biggest commitment I imagine a person ever makes—the family you choose to have forever. I haven't met that guy yet, but not for lack of desire to! I am moving to Austin soon and I would love someone to show me around.

HER STORY:

Theresa was never married and never lived with anyone, and had had an average number of both long-term and short-term relationships. In fact, she had had long stretches being single in between all her relationships, so this laid a good foundation for her to be generally happy. She was in her mid-thirties the first time she tried online dating, as she was on a quest to find someone to share her life with permanently; as she hit 39, she felt it was taking too long to find her ideal mate, so the Internet route seemed like her best solution.

Theresa looked into online dating for the first time when she lived in a "retirement city" and dating became more difficult because of the area's demographics. Despite the lack of younger people, she did have several dates there and learned the ropes quickly: always meeting in a public place, never letting a date pick her up at home on the first date, and having the initial meeting over coffee.

Theresa met some nice men, and also some not-so-nice men who seemed to be desperate for a hookup right off the bat. One guy, who looked pretty normal, went to her house to pick her up. (She made an exception with him to her dating rules because he was a friend of a friend.) She gave him the home tour, and as they passed each room he would say, "Is this where we're going to do it?" Each time she tried signing up for Match.com, after a month or two she just got discouraged and tired of the "merry-go-round" of it, so she'd hide her profile when the term was up.

She decided to move to Austin and get back on the "merry-go-round." Her new call to action was a line about her upcoming move, and that she would simply like to meet someone to tell her about the area. This line attracted a lot of men, even an actor, who suggested they have dinner at a popular Tex-Mex spot. After a long, uninterrupted monologue about himself while they were waiting for a table, the man made an unkind remark about a woman who walked past them and Theresa changed her mind about staying for the meal and left. After this date and also a few other unsuccessful ones earlier that week, she truly believed that her days of finding someone online were over. In general, she felt she was happy and had a good life, and had just about resigned herself to being single forever—and that that was really okay with her.

Theresa had decided she was done with online dating but she was going to keep one more date; the one she had set up before the one she walked out on. She had had good e-mail chemistry right off the bat with this other guy, also "on the move" to Austin, and he wanted to meet for lunch. Theresa thought it was ironic when Dan picked the same Tex-Mex restaurant where she had the bad "act" just the night before, but she agreed to meet him anyway—and that decision changed her life: They have a wonderful marriage today, six years later. Theresa believes that it's very likely that if it weren't for online dating, she and Dan would have never met, since they both work out of their homes and neither did a lot of bar hopping.

THERESA'S SILVER LINING:

She would tell you that her silver lining was everything that happened after the first few disastrous dates. The experiences led her to the perfect life partner and they are enjoying life in Austin to the fullest—like everyone else who moves there does!

THERESA'S BOTTOM LINE:

Have a "call to action" in your profile and propose a challenge to get men interested. Over a third of women go in and out of the dating groove but this time, her last, was by far her best move.

You *Can* Do Better

NORA'S PROFILE:

I am a 56-year-old widowed Southern woman. I love to cook, especially Cajun and Southern food. I am Catholic and a liberal and exercise regularly. I don't smoke, and don't want to date a smoker. I do, however, want to travel and am looking for a companion to spend time discovering Austin and all the unique things there are to do right around here.

HER STORY:

Nora, a widow, was married for nearly 40 years before finding herself single in her late fifties. Reluctant to date at first, she finally gave in to the idea of Internet dating two years later, when she found herself on a Friday night in her backyard alone, painting furniture that didn't even need painting. This was her tipping point as she looked down at her feet, covered with paint, and the thought washed over her: "Surely I can do better than this?"

With the help of a friend at work the next day, she was introduced to an online dating site and began the process. Her profile was a no-nonsense, honest one, with an initial statement that she was not after marriage but simply wanted to meet new people, have some fun, and maybe even get a few good dinners out of it along the way!

She got lots of dates at first, from "rednecks" to "royalty," and her story confirms that it does take kissing a lot of frogs before getting your prince. Her prince, "George," was a quiet man, also widowed, and reluctant to date, but an old high school friend bought him a membership and gave him no choice. Nora noticed his profile and was immediately intrigued by his innocent photo, which showed a baby stroller in the background. She realized after seeing this that he really did not know what he was doing. However, impressed by his innocence, she "winked" at him first, which was not her typical online dating protocol, and told him to call her.

Within a few days, George called her, and she could tell instantly by their conversation and the questions he asked her that he was a really good guy. In fact, he was the first man she dated who sent her flowers *before* their first date! Their dinner date took place at her favorite restaurant, which George selected, as he noted it was listed on Nora's profile. Her usual dating plan for a first date was to have a safe date and meet for coffee, but she knew something was different about this one from the beginning. When he picked her up that night, and she saw the sweetness in his eyes, she felt a deep attraction to this solid, smart, and handsome man.

Because this was George's first date in more than 30 years, since his wife died, Nora encouraged him to date other women for his own good. Although she did not date anyone else, he took her advice and went on one date, but came right back to her and said, "I know what I have." They were married about one year after they first met, although George proposed to her on her birthday, just one month after that first date. There was no hesitation at all to his early proposal, as she blurted out, "Yes," before he could even finish asking! They tied the knot in a small, quaint Catholic church in a remote section of the Bahamas, with the serene turquoise ocean as the perfect backdrop.

NORA'S SILVER LINING:

She recently got to purchase all new furniture for her backyard, because her old stuff eventually really did need painting, since she was too busy traveling to get to it!

NORA'S BOTTOM LINE:

Approach Internet dating with the attitude that you are a good catch. If you believe in both yourself and the process, and if you keep the faith even when it's challenged, you will find happiness.

The Handyman

BROOKE'S PROFILE:

A 40-year-old woman looking for a six-foot-tall, blond haired, athletic, and in-decent-physical-shape man who would make me the envy of all women. I would prefer someone without kids. I want someone with conservative views, not necessarily over-the-top but who would be a good family man. Someone with a real job (not working at McDonald's) and real goals for improvement in his life. I want someone who likes to go out on the town and enjoys being around people. I have always been a bit of a social butterfly, and I want someone who can keep up. Being an active, adventurous person is a must.

HER STORY:

Brooke had been married for two years to a man who left her feeling empty and worthless. Her husband, whose work schedule was nights and weekends—the opposite of hers—had an affair with a fellow employee. Brooke suspected something was up when she happened to see an e-mail from the other woman making references in a song about missing the smell of him on her pillow. He first denied it, saying that they often exchanged song lyrics, but Brooke retrieved the e-mail, put the pieces together, printed out the "customized" love song, and left it taped to their wedding picture. He asked for a divorce the next day, which happened to be exactly one day before what would have been their second wedding anniversary. Brooke had suggested they see a counselor first, but after one session he'd had enough. He not only filed for a swift divorce, he convinced Brooke that no one else would want her either—that she was unlovable, unattractive, and unworthy of anyone else's time or attention, and on top of all this, she was fat! This verbal bashing, and her unsuccessful attempts to meet anyone bar hopping, sent Brooke to an online dating site shortly after her divorce to boost her bruised ego. She had always felt it was creepy to meet anyone on the Internet, but for her, putting her profile out there helped fill a huge void, and at the same time made her feel wanted again as her unraveled life was slowly getting put back together.

Brooke found it uplifting to come home from work every day and see all the attention from interested men. To her, it was cheaper than therapy! She enjoyed corresponding with men through e-mails, and one man in particular caught her interest after several exchanges. They finally decided to meet in person, because she was anxious to get out of the house and was motivated to prove her ex-husband wrong. She was worthy of another man's attention, she could love and be loved again, and she wasn't fat! (If size 2 is considered fat, then I am in BIG trouble...)

She drove to meet Eric at a bar in north Austin. They had several drinks and great conversation, and even closed the bar down. Eric had a lot of the features Brooke was looking for: He was tall, fairly athletic, good-looking, and employed at a real job. In fact, he had just passed the bar exam and was working for a large law firm in town. On top of all this, he was even the head of a prestigious political group. Brooke was so excited about all the potential Eric seemingly had.

Their first date went well, and after a couple of drinks over pleasant and interesting conversation, it was time for both of them to go home, so he walked her to her car. Since they both seemed to connect, they willingly kissed in the parking lot. Brooke noticed a strange shaking going on during the kiss. It started off slowly at first, and then escalated just a bit during the short duration of the kiss. She felt a little uncomfortable, pulled away, and out of her peripheral vision saw Eric pull his hand out of his pants. He acted like nothing happened and asked her out again. She said she'd have to get back to him with her answer.

All the way home she kept thinking, and hoping, that what she thought she saw and felt was just a figment of her imagination. Brooke confided in a friend later, who thought it was funny and persuaded her go on a second date with the guy just to confirm her suspicions. So, reluctantly, Brooke met Eric at a restaurant, and then they went to a movie. Since they were close to his house after the movie, and since she was still hoping he had potential, they decided to go there for one last drink before calling it a night. She found herself getting a bit nervous as the date was ending and he wanted to kiss her before she left. As they were kissing at his front door, just like before, the shaking started. This time it was much more intentional and vigorous. She pulled away quickly and caught him in the act. His hand was in his pants and he was still moving it.

Brooke was stunned but decided to take the nonconfrontational, polite tactic of pretending it didn't happen. So she quickly said good night instead, got in her car, and immediately put "do not answer" next to his number. He eventually got the hint and stopped calling her.

MY TURN:
(I would have said this to Eric when I caught him in the act) Sorry to say I won't be seeing you again because it seems to me you've taken dating matters into your own hands! (And I would have put A REAL JERK next to his phone number.)

BROOKE'S SILVER LINING:
Brooke has learned to trust her instincts right off the bat and is convinced it's truly a woman's best built in radar that should rarely, if ever, be challenged! Being more judicious as she continued with her online dating gave her a lot more success with finding a match, proving to both herself and her ex-husband that his loss was another man's gain.

BROOKE'S BOTTOM LINE:
Trust your intuition, the first time.

Love Birds of a Feather...

JAN'S PROFILE:

I am looking for a male aged 52 to 63. I am athletic, slender, love the outdoors, dress-up occasions, and dancing. I would like my match to be fit, healthy, and show success and happiness in his career. I am a Christian and would prefer the same. I enjoy giving and attending dinner parties. My ideal match would have a passion for something outside of his own life and give unto others—it doesn't matter what in particular. I volunteer my time to dance and environmental projects, music at church, and to a state agency, of which I am a board member. Although I work in and own my own business, I can still find plenty of time for a special romance.

HER STORY:

Jan, now in her early 50s, was married for 19 years. She knew early on that the marriage wouldn't last, but tried to stick it out until their two children got older. For a variety of reasons, she couldn't follow through with that plan.

Jan spent most of her time and energy after the divorce on work and her kids. Once she felt her kids were on their way with their lives, she decided to play the "dating game." She had some pretty humorous dates at first, and the one she still laughs about was with a guy who "shuffled" into a very nice bar to meet her dressed in ragged shorts, a tacky floral beach shirt, white calf-length socks, and black

Keds! Even the bartender tried to save her from the horrible date, after they both saw how rude he was by certain comments he made, and let her slip out of the bar while the date was in the restroom. The bartender even made up a lie for her sudden exit when her date returned.

She had other dates and learned quickly to discern between what was listed on someone's profile and what it really meant. (Jan gave me the idea for the *Handy Dandy Internet Profile Decoder*.) Several years past and finally all the unsuccessful dates led her to a guy who would change her loneliness. She noticed instantly that she and Sam had a lot in common. It was almost eerie, she thought. They were comfortable enough through both phone calls and e-mail exchanges using the dating site to start communicating with their real e-mail addresses. It was here that she discovered she knew this man from her same line of work and had nothing but the greatest respect for him as a professional. Jan told Sam that she would be at her church on a Sunday, playing with the music group, and he showed up there. In fact, within ten minutes she recognized him from his profile picture. Little did she know that her church was his church as well! They met after the service briefly and set up a second date at Luby's for lunch.

She was thrilled to know and date this man, especially since Jan already had respect for Sam's work, and his professional credentials put her at ease. Since he traveled a lot, they decided to take things slowly. She was dating two others when she met "the one," but over time took her profile off and put all her energy into Sam. Being a bit old-fashioned, she waited until her last kid was out of the house before the relationship became more serious.

Two years later, at five o'clock one morning, Jan got a text from Sam that said, "What is your ring size?" The formal proposal, however, took place while she and her mom were visiting him and his daughter at his summer place a few weeks later. He pulled out the ring and in front of the whole group asked for her hand in marriage. Ahh . . . how sweet (and confident) of him.

JAN'S SILVER LINING:

Jan turned around her disastrous start to Internet dating by taking some time off from it for a while—like the other third of women who do this—and then getting back into it when she was ready. Her new approach to use very specific filters, learn how to decode men's profiles and a change in her attitude paid off. She and Sam have a wonderful life together, and their circle will be complete at year's end, when they both retire and make his summer home their permanent residence.

JAN'S BOTTOM LINE:

You will have far more success attracting the right person by finding someone who shares your same interests and values. And do learn to "decode" some of the men's profiles—it will save you a lot of time and energy!

My Bottom Line

NOW, LOOKING BACK AT MY 18 months collecting stories from women about their dating experiences, I see it was an amazing journey. The women I interviewed reached out to me in a very special way because I was an active and interested listener, even though some of the women were strangers. By listening, I felt I helped these women who needed to vent. I was baffled by the research on Internet dating that revealed there is a huge disconnect between what men worry about (according to Randomhistory.com) and what worries women. Although my title implies women are concerned with their size in comparison to their dates, in reality some women worry about dating a serial killer while it's the men who worry they'll be matched up with someone fat!

I felt that everyone I met took something positive away from their online dating experience. One woman told me that she would have never met the female friends she did if she hadn't signed up on a dating site where she met a man who told her about a fitness club, which she eventually joined, and she now cherishes all the women friends she has met there. Although the guy is history, she looks great from working out, and her life is fuller than ever! One woman dated a guy who would cut their dates short by telling her that his grandmother died. The only problem was that the grandmother died at least three, maybe four, times? All she could say to me after getting wise to him was "that poor grandmother!"

People have asked me why I sought out these stories. So many of my friends were now dating, and I found myself fascinated with other women's dating tales. Getting their stories answered a question I had: How has the dating world changed? And what started for me as "match.comedy" evolved into more like "match.hope" and then ultimately "match.help", all of which I felt compelled to share.

I was not really expecting to hear the shocking stories I did, nor the sweet ones, but in the end they formed a perfect blend of experiences. After hours of listening to every dating detail, running up both my Starbucks tab and cell phone bill, passing up on golf games and tennis matches, and aggravating my arthritic hands from all the note taking and typing, how satisfying that I received my own silver lining in an e-mail sent to me after one of my interviews:

> "I want to feel like you do about your husband after 30 years of marriage. I want to like him; I want to enjoy his company; I want to respect the kind of parent and person he is. If I can't have that then I will just stay single. From my Internet dating experiences, I am truly learning to embrace singlehood."

And finally, when I think about all the brave women I've talked to this past year and a half, I realize they're all on the same path—to also find their silver lining, or happy ending, to online dating; and while they think they are LOOKING for a match, I see that they are really FINDING themselves. It's been an awesome process to take part in.

Got a good story to share?
I want to hear from you!

Please visit my website:
www.cathyromano.com

38267228R00047

Made in the USA
Charleston, SC
03 February 2015